BE INSPIRED

DEDICATION

"My dear Aaron Justice Fryer, this book is a dedication to you. Losing you was one of the most difficult things I have ever had to endure. Your passing may have caused immense pain, but it also brought about a tremendous amount of inspiration. You never gave up in life, and your resilience has become an inspiration to all of us. As you continue to live on in our hearts, I want to extend my gratitude to all those who have purchased this book. Your support means everything to me. Remember to never give up on your journey, no matter how challenging it may seem."

BE INSPIRED

If a homeless person can sleep in the woods inside of a tent and get up every morning to beg for money in the rain, sleet, and snow, who am I to complain? It is just that simple.

BE INSPIRED

"Inhale, exhale
through the
difficulties of life.
Push through the
pain and continue to
fight. That's life."

BE INSPIRED

"When you move out
of your way,

blessings will happen.

Let the universe
guide your steps."

BE INSPIRED

"Stop putting off yesterday for tomorrow and waiting for the right time. Neither of those may ever come."

BE INSPIRED

"Sometimes you must step back and focus your lenses. Then, move on."

BE INSPIRED

"The early bird gets the worm. If you are earlier than that, you get the whole bird."

BE INSPIRED

"It is time to stop chasing your dreams and start living them by any means necessary."

BE INSPIRED

"The world could be yours if you just give some effort. Do not waste time; you can never get it back."

BE INSPIRED

"When you feel like you are drowning, take a deep breath, step back. 1, 2, 3, 4, 5, 6, 7, 8, 9, 10. Now, you can swim."

BE INSPIRED

"I will never turn my
back on the galaxy,
but that bullshit
meets my back."

BE INSPIRED

"Every time the storm comes, push through it. Strength is within you to make it."

BE INSPIRED

"Sometimes, when you do what's right, people may perceive it as wrong. However, as long as God knows your heart, never stop doing what's right."

BE INSPIRED

"Let the haters hate.
It is their destiny.
Those who genuinely
love you accept their
energy."

BE INSPIRED

"Do not think about it, be about it. Life is too short not to achieve your dreams."

BE INSPIRED

"No matter what,
keep pushing through
the pain. There's
greatness on the
other side."

BE INSPIRED

"Success is obtained by success.

It would be best if you succeeded in being successful.

Take the steps you need to take to get where you want to be."

BE INSPIRED

"With the right
people behind you,
you never have to
worry about what,
when, where, or who.
They are always
there."

BE INSPIRED

"Ayo poet, what steps
are you taking to
reach your dreams?"

BE INSPIRED

"I miss you every day, Grandmother. I hope I am making you proud."

BE INSPIRED

"I am proud of you.
Keep doing what you
are doing. Self-love
talk is necessary."

BE INSPIRED

"Sometimes you will doubt yourself. Shake it off, then keep going."

BE INSPIRED

"Even in my darkness, my light shines. They are trying to stop me. They did not get the memo: I murdered 'try.'"

BE INSPIRED

"When we stand together, we cannot lose. Pick your brother up when he falls; do not step on him."

BE INSPIRED

"The Galaxy is on the rise. Are you all ready? I know you are. To the Galaxy!"

BE INSPIRED

"My heart cannot wait for you to figure out if I am important enough."

BE INSPIRED

I bring the heat, turn it into ether, and flame it on. Flame is ignited infinity times infinity.

(New intro)

My soul speaks the words that were spoken to me, so listen.

BE INSPIRED

"We will forever love and miss you, Dad. Saying 'Happy Father's Day' to other fathers has a sting."

BE INSPIRED

"Clarity comes in different ways. What is yours? Find it and focus on it."

BE INSPIRED

"Some people hate it when you are no longer caught up in the procrastination of life. Oh well, note to self: keep rising!"

BE INSPIRED

"My heart is heavy,
but I am happy. It has
been a good morning.
Live, love, spread
charity, and be
grateful."

BE INSPIRED

"I see your future.
You look good."

BE INSPIRED

"The day I murdered
try and killed can't
was the day I
defeated won't."

BE INSPIRED

"Some people say they are family. You, whom I hardly know, showed me what family means. Thank you."

BE INSPIRED

"Life can change in a second. Always be prepared."

BE INSPIRED

"When you stay humble, God will handle your problems."

BE INSPIRED

"Walking soothes my soul. Counting calms my heartbeat. Silence is bliss for my mind."

BE INSPIRED

"Support goes a long way, and you do not have to pay anything for it."

BE INSPIRED

"F**k a New Year's resolution, let us build a network like they've never seen before."

BE INSPIRED

"When a wall is put in front of you, and it is too high to climb, too deep to dig under, too long to the right and the left to go around it, what do you do? Go through it."

BE INSPIRED

"Black men do not
say it enough. I love
you, black man."

BE INSPIRED

"Always remember, people will change even when you think they have grown. They will turn around to show you the devil that is inside of them."

BE INSPIRED

"My mind creates peace. I silence the noise to mold my reality into what I need it to be physically."

BE INSPIRED

"You are all amazing,
wonderful souls, and I
am grateful to have
you on this journey
with me. Though we
may face adversity,
we will conquer it
together, always
supporting each
other from every
angle. You are my
rock, and your
unwavering support

BE INSPIRED

keeps me going.
Remember, we are
strong individuals
alone, but together
we are unstoppable.
Let us pray often,
manifest often, and
forever love one
another. Together,
we can reach for the
stars and achieve
greatness. To The
Galaxy."

BE INSPIRED

Death came knocking for me, and I almost answered; however, I had pillars holding me up. For them, I am thankful.

BE INSPIRED

"In closing, I would
like to leave you with
this: there is nothing
you cannot do in life
if you push through
adversity.
You will make it
through."

BE INSPIRED

YOU ARE DOPE
YOU ARE GREAT
YOU ARE YOU
YOU ARE PURPOSE
BE INSPIRED